STAY CONNECTED WITH

twitter and insta

www.dramenon.com

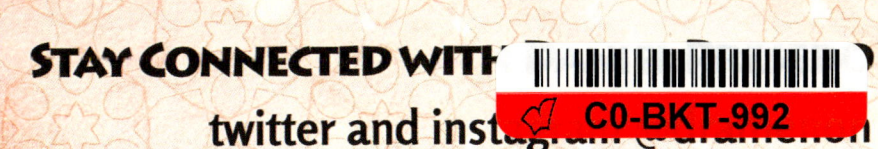

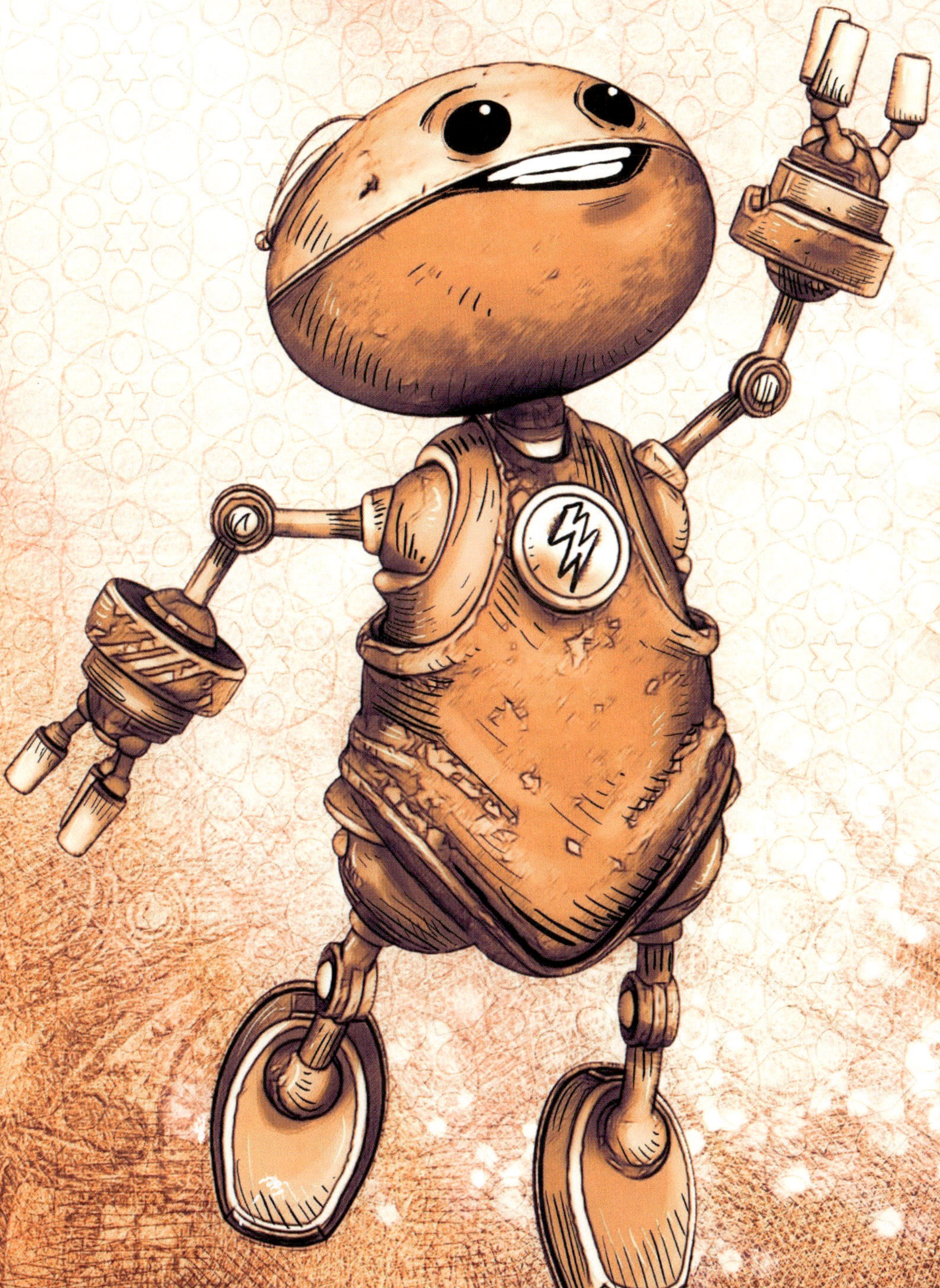

Life of Robots ™

WRITTEN AND ILLUSTRATED
BY DANIEL PRESEDO

Editing assists by
Kai & Alicia

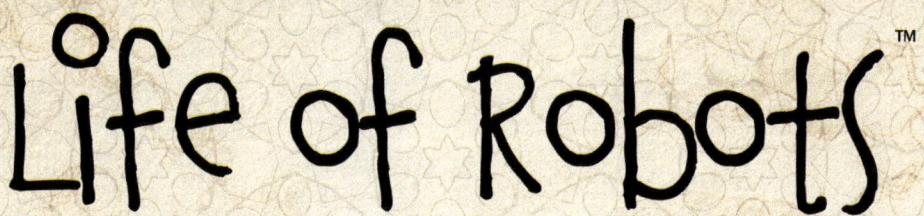

To be, or not to be, that is the question . . .

Hi, my name is Archimedes
and I am a Robot!

I was programmed by the
author of this book to tell you
about the Life of Robots.

Most humans believe that robots are a
recent invention. However, our history
goes back over 2000 years!

For example, Archytas made his
robot-bird over 2,000 years ago.

This bird was able to fly
about 200 meters before
it ran out of steam.

Did you know there are more than a million robots used all over the world today?

Half of them can be found in a variety of places including hospitals, labs, and energy plants.

In fact, simple robotic technology can be found in your toys!

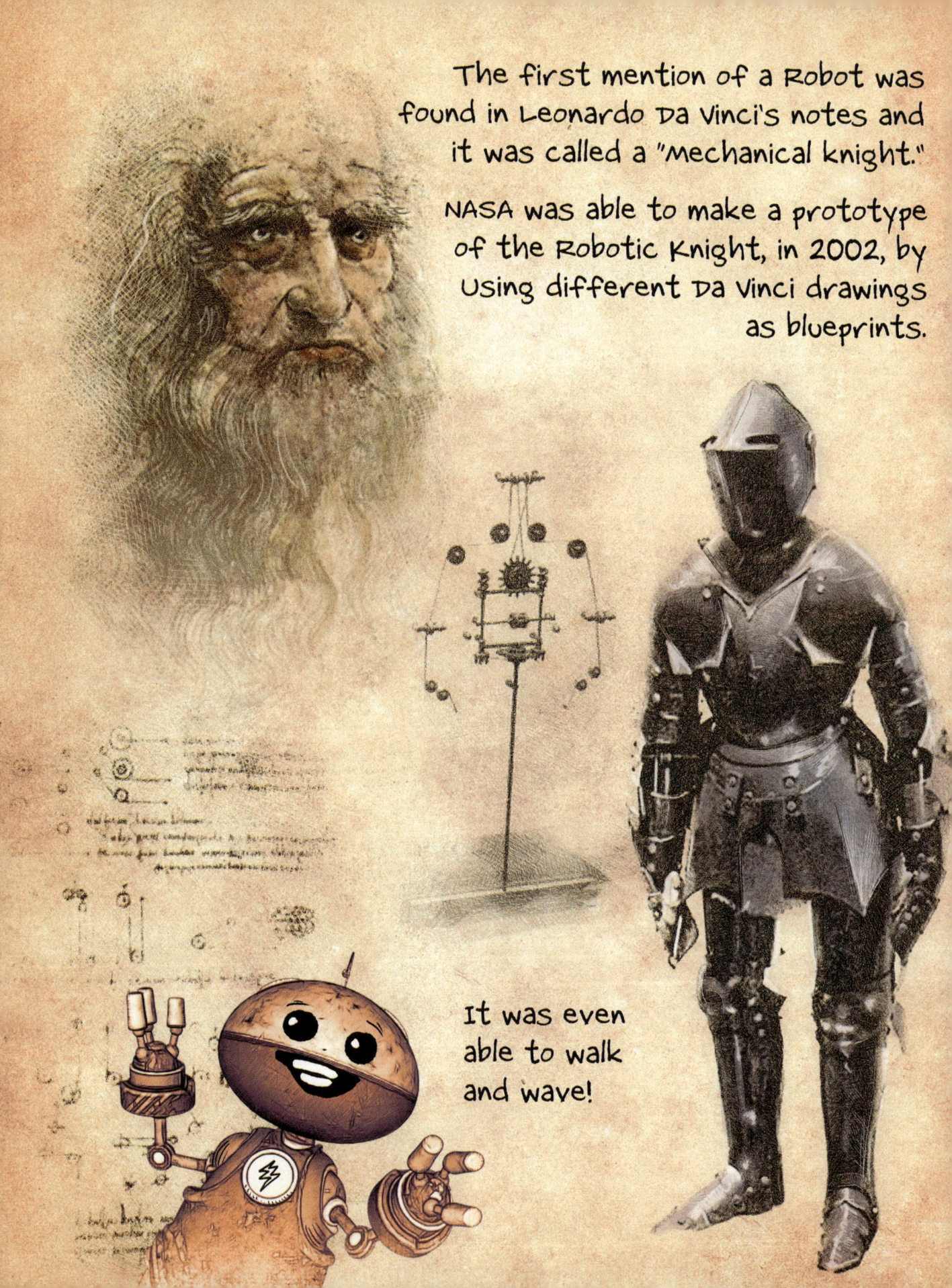

The first mention of a Robot was found in Leonardo Da Vinci's notes and it was called a "mechanical knight."

NASA was able to make a prototype of the Robotic Knight, in 2002, by using different Da Vinci drawings as blueprints.

It was even able to walk and wave!

The word Robot was introduced by Czech playwright, novelist and journalist Karel Capek.

He introduced the Robot in 1920 for his hit play "Rossum's Universal Robots."

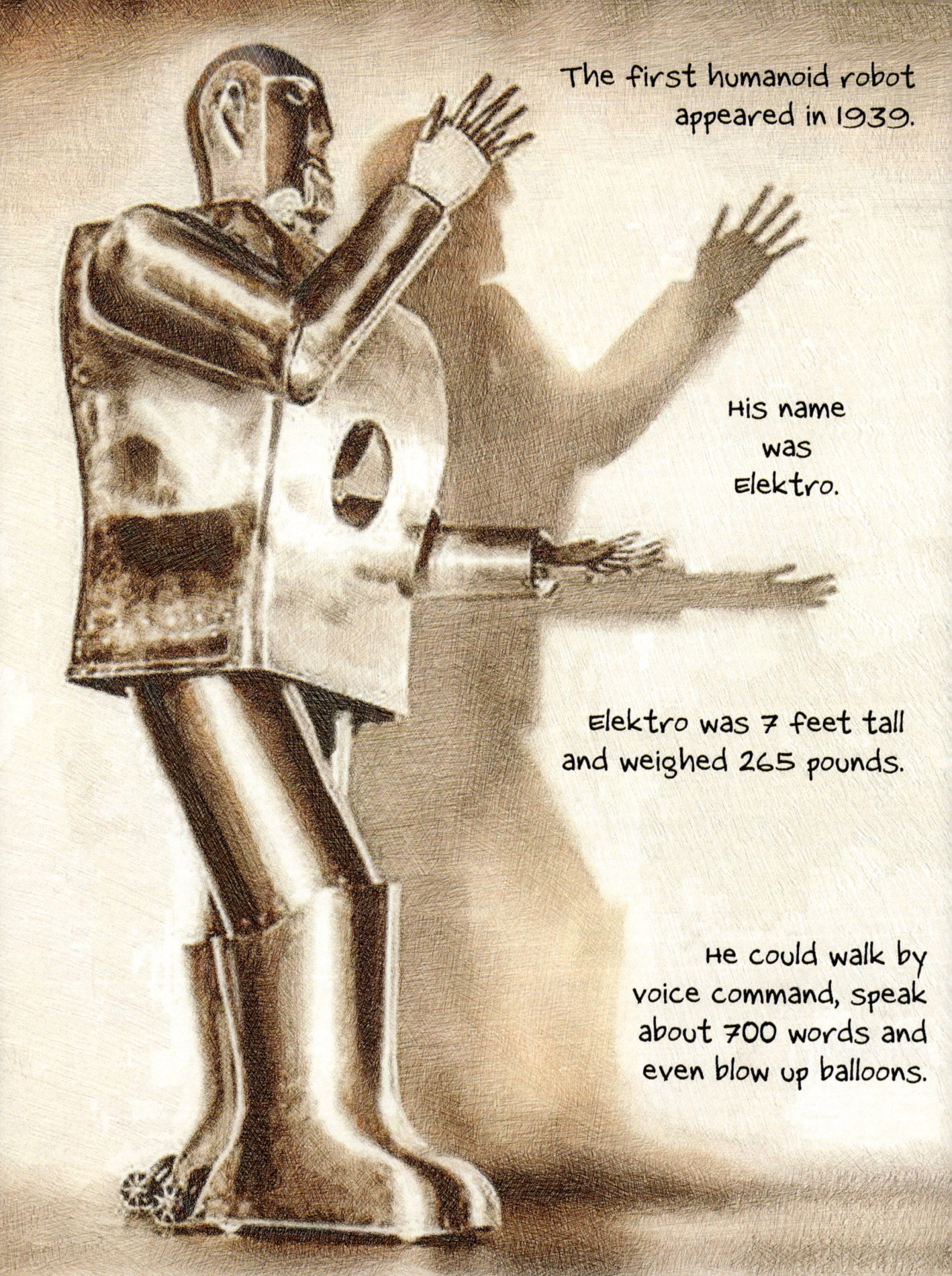

The first humanoid robot appeared in 1939.

His name was Elektro.

Elektro was 7 feet tall and weighed 265 pounds.

He could walk by voice command, speak about 700 words and even blow up balloons.

The first robot TOY was produced during the 1940's in Japan.

The 'Lilliput' was a wind-up toy which walked. It was made from tinplate and stood just a little over 5.5 inches tall.

Do your parents have any Robots that look like this?

Science fiction writer Isaac Asimov, in 1941, writes the short story 'Liar!' in which he describes the Three Laws of Robotics.

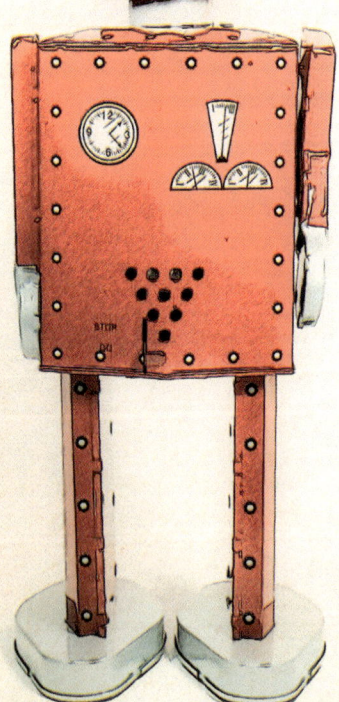

1. A robot may not injure a human being or, through inaction, allow a human being to come to harm.

2. A robot must obey any orders given to it by human beings, except where such orders would conflict with the First Law.

3. A robot must protect its own existence as long as such protection does not conflict with the First or Second Law.

I am glad there were only 3!

The next toy robot was Atomic Robot Man in the late 1940's.

Robots do not always look like a human.

The world's first working robot joined the assembly line in 1961. It helped to assemble cars!

How many different cars have you seen today?

In 1964 the first mass produced computer comes from IBM! It was called the 360.

Not to be confused with the much smaller and more powerful Microsoft XBox 360!

Imagine the IBM 360 fitting in your home!

This punch card was the typical way for inputting information into an old computer.

In 1969 the U.S.A. successfully landed on the moon!

They used the latest in computing, robotic and space technology for this achievement.

There are many types of Robots. Let's start with –

Domestic Robots

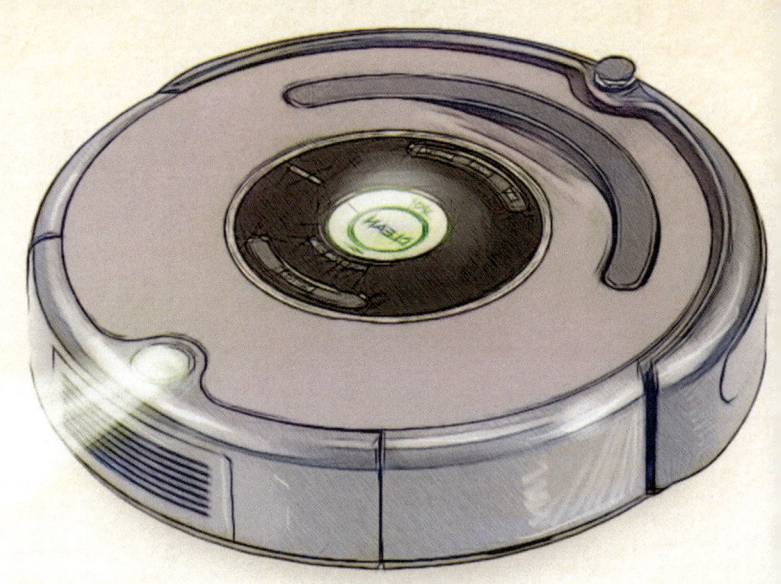

These include Robots used at a home like a vacum cleaner or pool cleaners. These Robots can move around you.

Industrial Robots

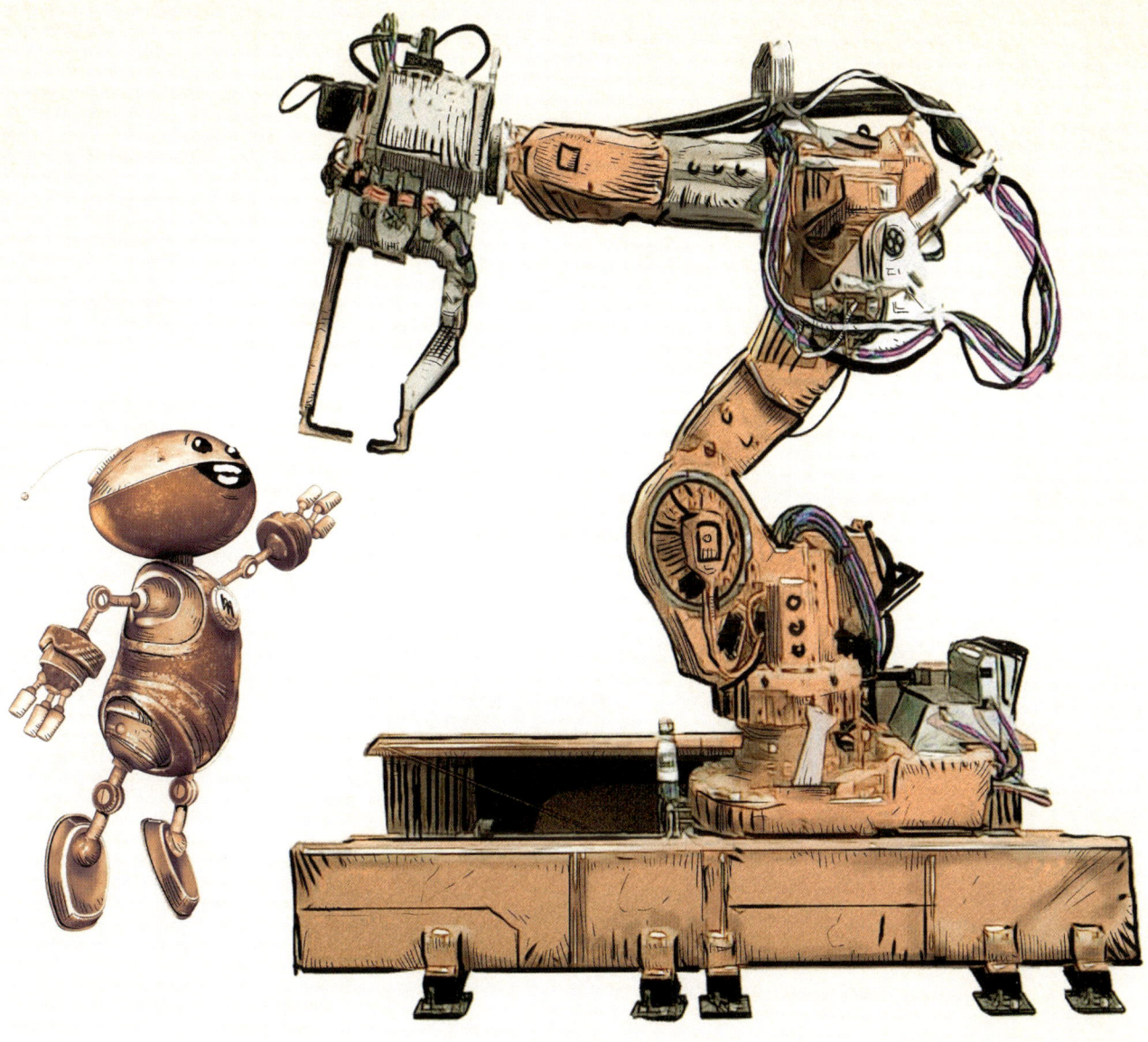

These Robots are used in manufacturing and have a jointed arm that is attached to a fixed surface. They might do welding, picking things up, painting and others repetitive tasks.

Medical Robots

Beginning in 2017 the Da Vinci X system will provide surgeons and hospitals with access to some of the most advanced robotic-assisted surgery technology.

I don't know if I am ready for this!

I might feel more comfortable with just a mechanic!

Educational Robots

 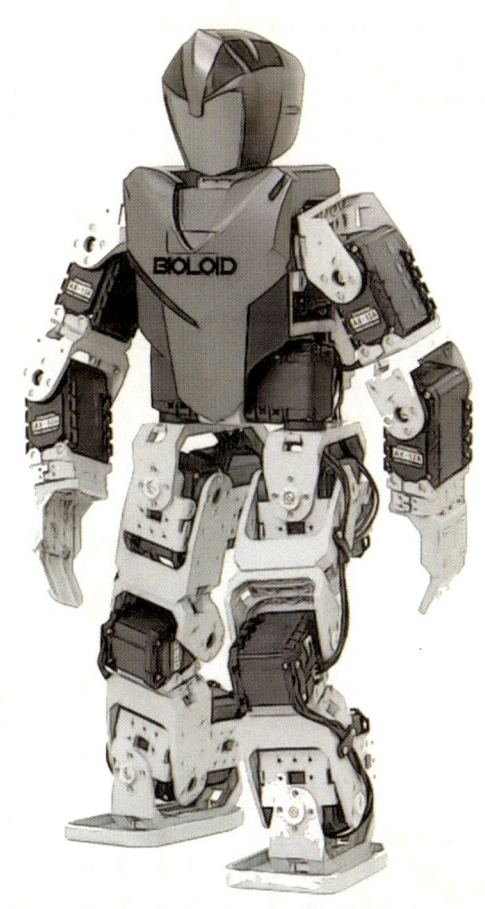

There are robot kits like Lego Mindstorms, BIOLOID, or BotBrain Educational Robots that can help children to learn about mathematics, physics, programming, and electronics.

Military Robots

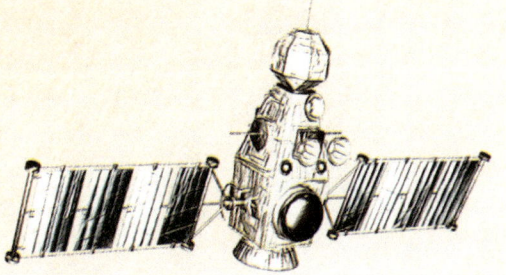

Some orbit
around us way
over our heads!

Other remote controlled mobile robots are
designed for the military.

They can be used for
transport, search and
rescue or attack.

Entertainment Robots

These Robots can safely and effectively interact with humans.

Amusement parks like Disneyland and Universal Studios use a lot of Robots!

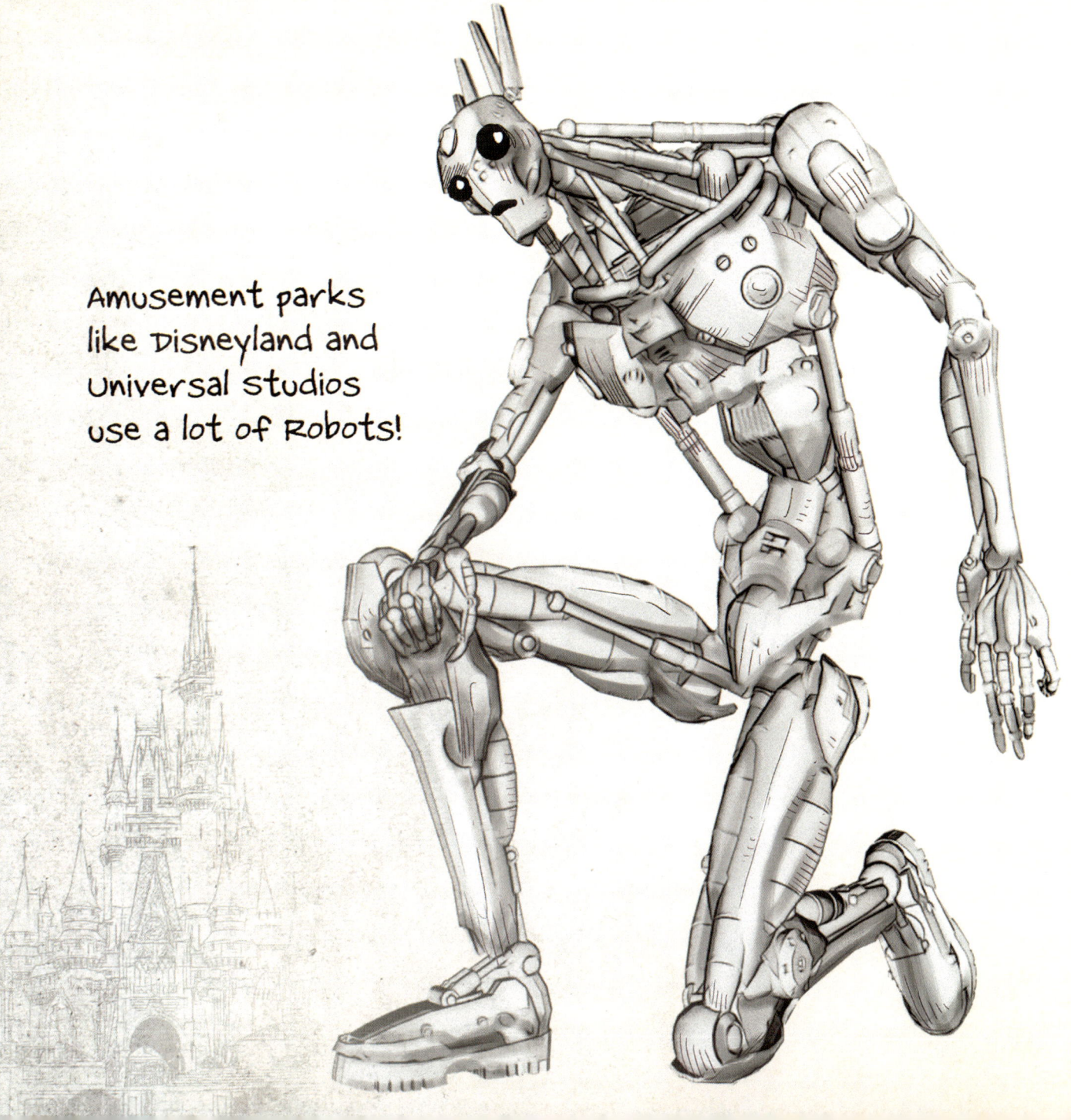

Whew! That was a lot of information, I think I need to re-charge.

How do you re-charge?

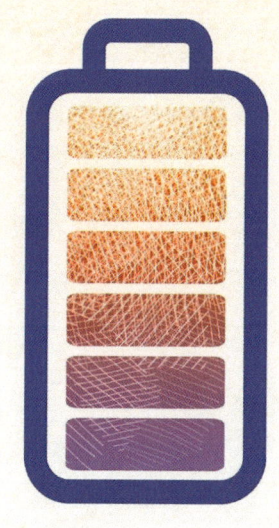

Can you name one source of renewable energy?

Renewable Energy is energy generated from natural resources.

Ok let's keep going!

A space probe is a robotic spacecraft that does not orbit the Earth, but instead, explores further into outer space!

NASA's Mars Exploration Rover mission is an ongoing robotic space mission involving two Mars rovers. There names are Spirit and Opportunity, exploring the planet Mars.

A Mars rover is an automated motor vehicle that propels itself across the surface of the planet!

Swarm Robots

These are inspired by colonies of insects such as ants and bees!

Scientist are modeling the behavior of swarms of thousands of tiny robots to perform a useful task.

There are many more Robots that do a
variety of things around us and for us.

How do they do some of these things?
Artificial Intelligence or A.I. !

Artificial Intelligence is intelligence
demonstrated by machines.

I think, therefore I am.

Nanotechnology

Nanorobotics, Nanomachines, nanobots ...

Nanorobotics is a technology field creating machines or robots with components that are very, very small.

They usually range in sizes equal to one billionth of a meter (0.000000001 meter.)

A Nanorobot could fit inside a SINGLE CELL!

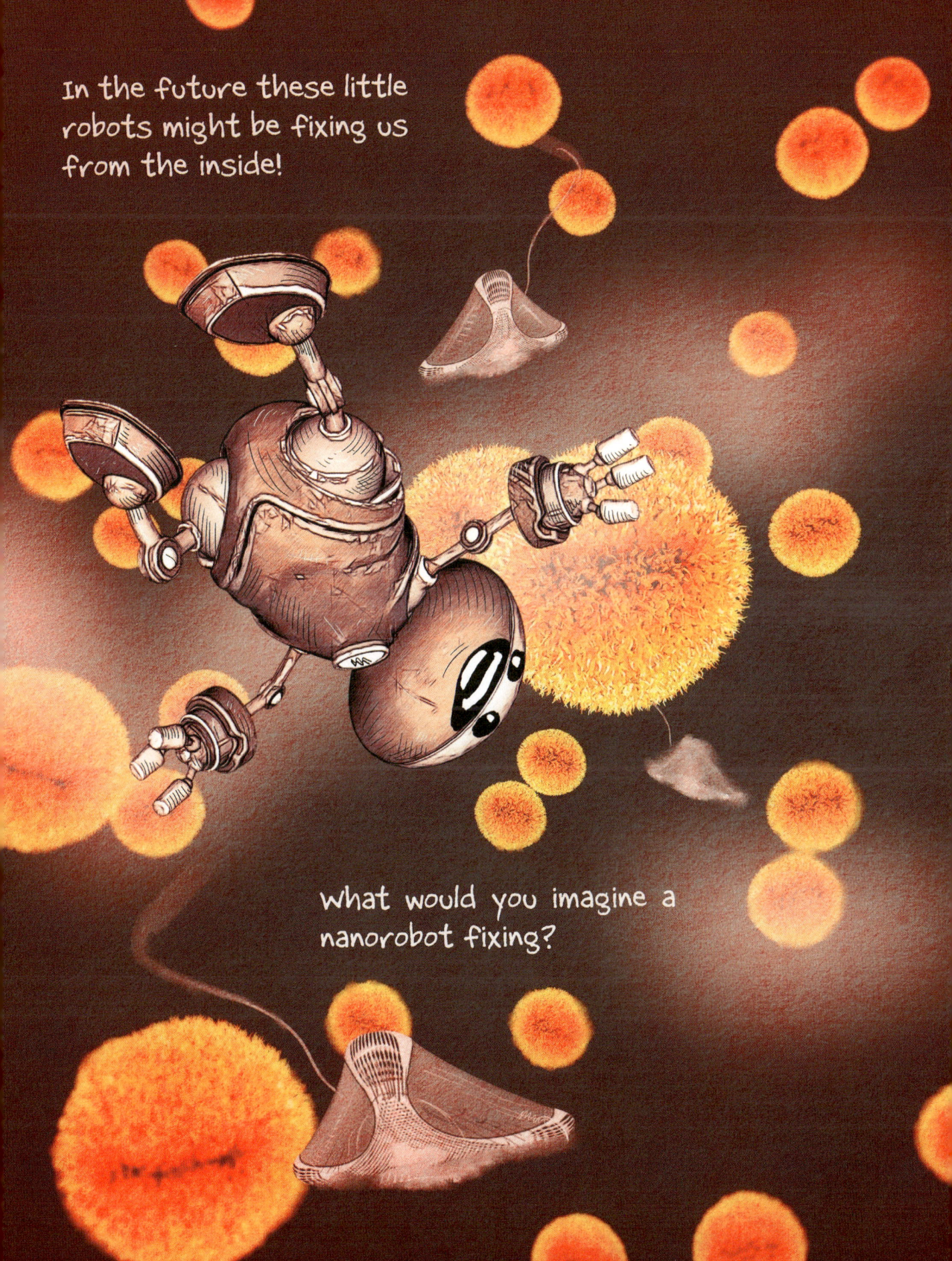

In the future these little robots might be fixing us from the inside!

what would you imagine a nanorobot fixing?

Time to use our imaginations! Think of all the robots you may have seen or read about.

How many of these robots do you recognize?

Who wants to invent something new? Do you want to create a show starring your very own Robots?

maybe YOU will write the next great ROBOT Tale!

I hope this has helped you think
about how Robots, like me, fit in
this world –

– Big and small, useful
or entertaining.

You don't need to be an adult to start building your first robot.

You just have to have the desire.

students of all ages have designed, created, and programed their own robots.

with the right resources and tools,
anyone can build a basic robot.

Find some pencils, or pens and
start designing and thinking...

what kind of Robot
would you build?

Made in the USA
Columbia, SC
07 August 2017